ST JAMES C of E PRIMARY SCHOOL
Thursley Road
Elstead
Surrey GU8 6DH

POWER FROM WATER

Hazel Songhurst

Other titles in this series include:
Power from the Earth
Power from Plants
Power from the Sun
Power from the Wind

Cover: The force of the sea contains a lot of energy.

Editor: Deb Elliott

Designer: David Armitage

Text is based on *Water Energy* in the Alternative Energy series published in 1990.

Picture acknowledgements
J. Allan Cash Picture Library 4 (left), 5, 6, 7 (above), 26; Bruce Coleman 8; Energy Technology Support Unit 12, 16, 24 (right); Environmental Picture Library 17 (above); Geoscience Features Picture Library 4 (right); National Power 11; Oxford Scientific Films 7 (below); Photri 18; Science Photo Library 24 (left); Snowy Mountains Hydro-Electric Authority 22 (right), 25; Tony Stone Worldwide 23; Tasmanian Hydro-Electric Commission 9; Topham Picture Library 17 (below); United States Department of Energy 22 (left); Zefa Picture Library 14. All the artwork is by Nick Hawken.

First published in 1993 by
Wayland (Publishers) Limited
61 Western Road, Hove
East Sussex BN3 1JD

British Library Cataloguing in Publication Data
Songhurst, Hazel
Power from Water. - (Energy Series)
I.Title II.Series
ISBN 0 7502 0720 5

Typeset by Perspective Marketing Limited

Printed in Italy by G. Canale & C.S.p.A.

Contents

Energy	4
The energy in water	6
Tides	10
Waves	14
Heat from the sea	18
Hydroelectric power	21
Making a water-wheel	28
Glossary	30
Books to read	31
Index	32

Energy

This boat is clearing up oil that has been spilled into the sea. Oil kills fish, seabirds and other wildlife and washes up on to beaches.

These trees have been killed by acid rain. This is caused by poisonous gases sent into the air when coal, oil and gas (fossil fuels) are burned.

POWER FROM WATER

This power station in Romania uses coal as fuel. Look how much smoke is pouring out into the air.

We make the electricity we need by burning fossil fuels - coal, oil or gas. But supplies of fossil fuels are starting to run out. They are also harming our environment. Now, scientists are looking at new ways to make the power we need.

The energy in water

The water in oceans, rivers, streams and waterfalls is always moving. Moving energy is called kinetic energy. The energy in water could be trapped and used to make electricity.

The photograph below was taken in space. It shows a view of the Earth. The darkest areas are the Pacific (left) and Atlantic (right) Oceans.

POWER FROM WATER

There are huge amounts of kinetic energy in the rushing water of this waterfall.

Can you see the river water flowing over this water-wheel? The power of the water makes the wheel turn.

POWER FROM WATER

This water-wheel powers a hammer that shapes metal.

Water-wheels worked the machines in the first factories more than 200 years ago.

Today, people are trying to find new ways to trap the energy in water. Hydroelectric power schemes use falling water from rivers or reservoirs to make electricity. A reservoir is a lake made by people. It is made by building a dam across a river.

Opposite *The Gordon Dam in Tasmania has formed a huge reservoir.*

POWER FROM WATER

Tides

Every day the level of water in the Earth's oceans rises and falls. We call these movements tides.

The water moves about because it is pulled by a powerful force given out by the Sun and the Moon. This powerful force is called gravity.

These diagrams show how the level of the tides changes as the Moon goes round the Earth.

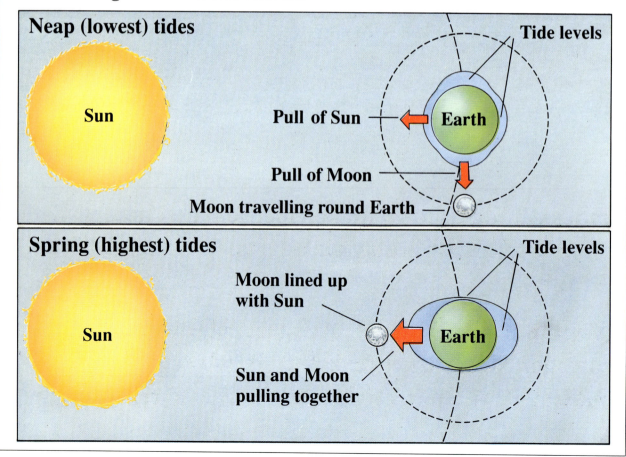

POWER FROM WATER

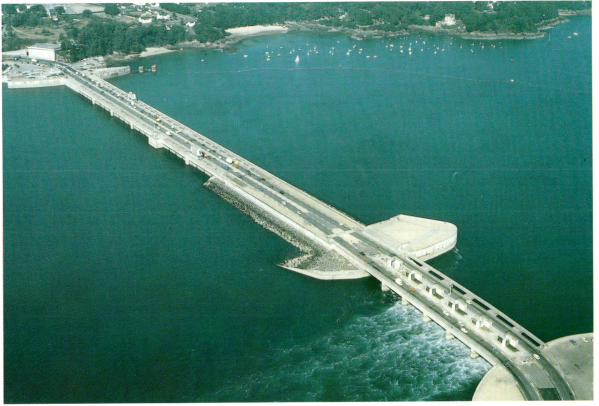

This barrage stretches across the River Rance in France.

Tides can be used to make electricity. A long wall called a barrage is built across a wide estuary. This is the highest part of the river where it meets the sea.

When the tide is high, water gets trapped behind the barrage. When the tide is low, it is let out through machines called turbines that make electricity.

POWER FROM WATER

This drawing shows where a tidal power station could be built across the estuary of the River Severn in Britain.

The barrage would be 18 kilometres long with 216 turbines.

Tidal barrages make electricity cheaply and they are easy to run. But there are some problems, too. Building them is difficult and costs a lot of money. They cannot always make power when it is most needed because high and low tides come at different times every day.

The diagram opposite shows how a tidal barrage works.

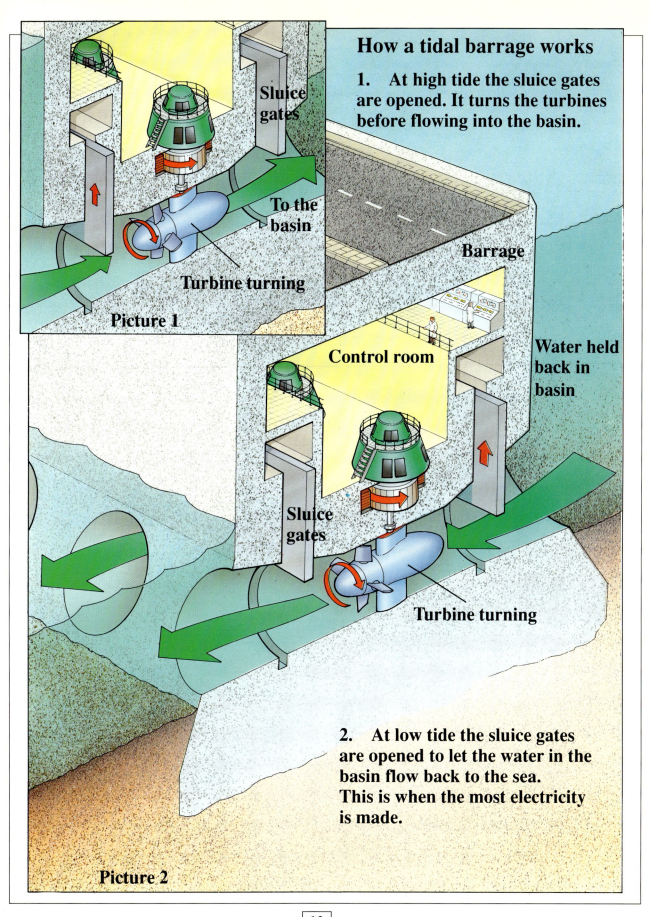

Waves

When winds blow over the oceans they whip up waves. The biggest waves can be 25 metres high.

Waves are full of powerful kinetic energy. Scientists are trying to build machines to trap this energy.

The best wave machines have a moving column of water inside them. The waves rise and fall and force the column up and down. This movement pushes air through a turbine to work a machine which makes electricity.

This huge wave is full of kinetic energy.

The diagram opposite shows how a wave machine works.

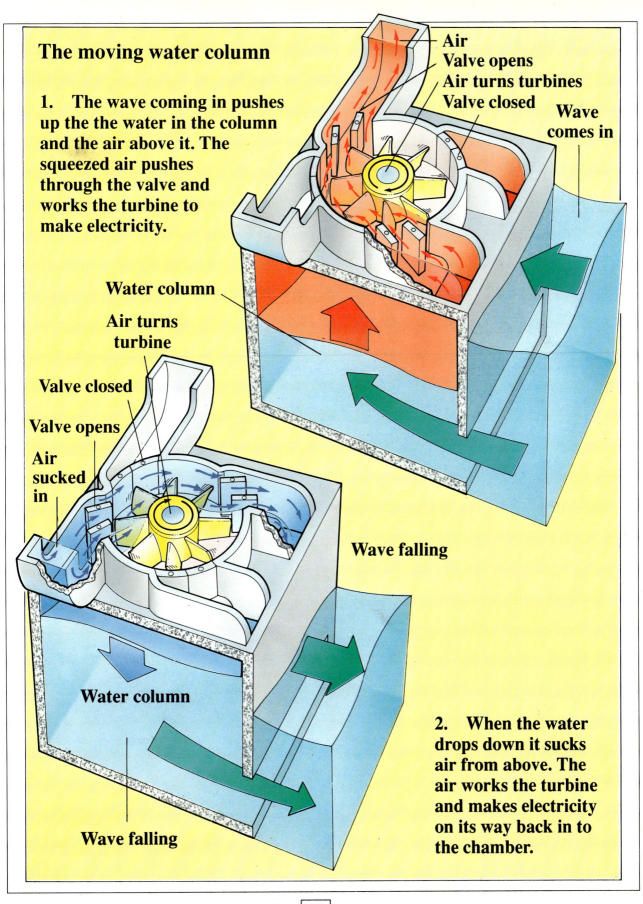

POWER FROM WATER

Wave machines have been built in the seas off Norway and Japan. They are difficult to build because they must be strong enough to stand being battered by the wind and waves.

This drawing shows a design for a power station that will get power from rows of wave machines.

POWER FROM WATER

This wave machine in Norway is built on a cliff. It is one of the most modern machines in the world.

Stormy seas like this have damaged wave machines. New ones must be even more strongly built.

Heat from the sea

In hot countries the sea is much warmer than in cold countries. The surface of the sea stores up heat from the Sun.

A swim in this tropical ocean would be like a swim in a warm bath!

Warm sea water is used to heat a liquid and change it into gas. The gas powers a turbine that makes electricity.

Cold sea water changes the gas back to liquid so it can be used again.

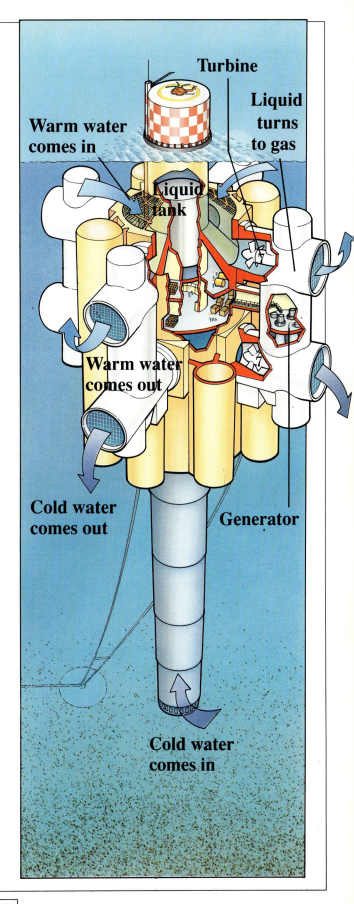

This drawing shows a machine called an Ocean Energy Thermal Conversion Unit. It uses heat from the sea to make electricity.

POWER FROM WATER

This drawing shows you how a hydroelectric power (HEP) scheme works.

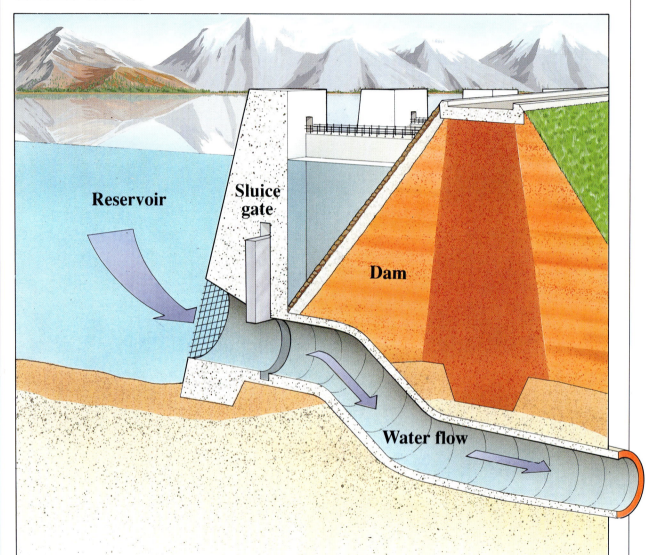

The dam holds back the water in the reservoir. When the sluice gate opens it lets water into the tunnel. The water gathers speed as it flows downhill. It spins the turbine and drives the generator to make electricity.

Hydroelectric power

Water that flows downhill, such as in mountain rivers or streams, is full of energy. Hydroelectric power (HEP) schemes use this falling water to make electricity.

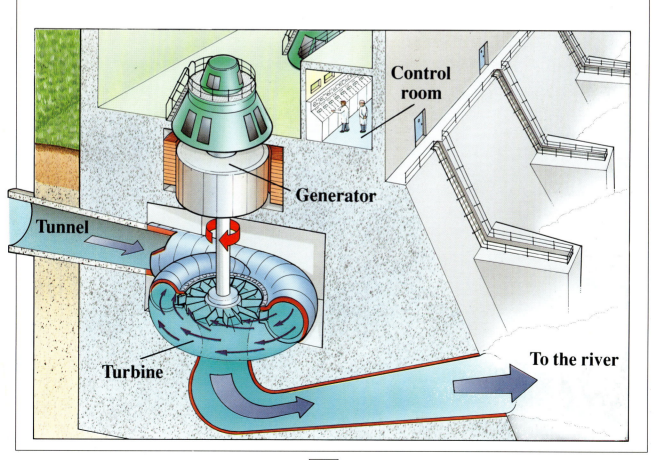

POWER FROM WATER

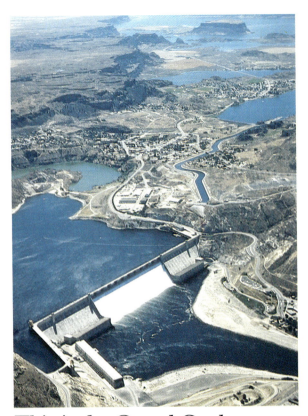

This is the Grand Coulee Dam in the USA. It is 170 metres high. The HEP station here supplies electricity to thousands of homes.

You can see the tops of the generators inside this HEP station. Stations are easy to run, and only a few people work in them.

We will never run out of power from falling water. New supplies are made every time it rains or snows.

POWER FROM WATER

Many developing countries are being helped to build their own HEP schemes by developed countries, such as the USA and Britain.

Sometimes, when a river is dammed, large areas of land are flooded, which damages plants and wildlife. But HEP schemes also bring water for growing crops to hot, dry lands.

Water from an HEP scheme is sprayed over crops.

POWER FROM WATER

This is the Dinorwic power station in North Wales. It has been named the 'Electric Mountain' because the water it uses falls through tunnels dug through a mountain.

This turbine is part of a small HEP station. It could make electricity for communities (small groups of people), such as people who live on small islands.

POWER FROM WATER

The Snowy Mountains scheme

The biggest HEP scheme in the world is in Australia. It is in the Snowy Mountains. Hundreds of rivers and streams flow down this mountain range. It is the only 'wet' area of Australia.

Building the Snowy Mountains scheme.

POWER FROM WATER

The 'Snowy' scheme is huge - there are sixteen dams and seven power stations! Water from four rivers falls hundreds of metres through tunnels, shafts and pipes. It makes thousands of megawatts of electricity and supplies water for farmland.

__Opposite page__ This drawing shows part of the Snowy Mountains scheme.

The water in these pipes falls 450 metres to the power station below.

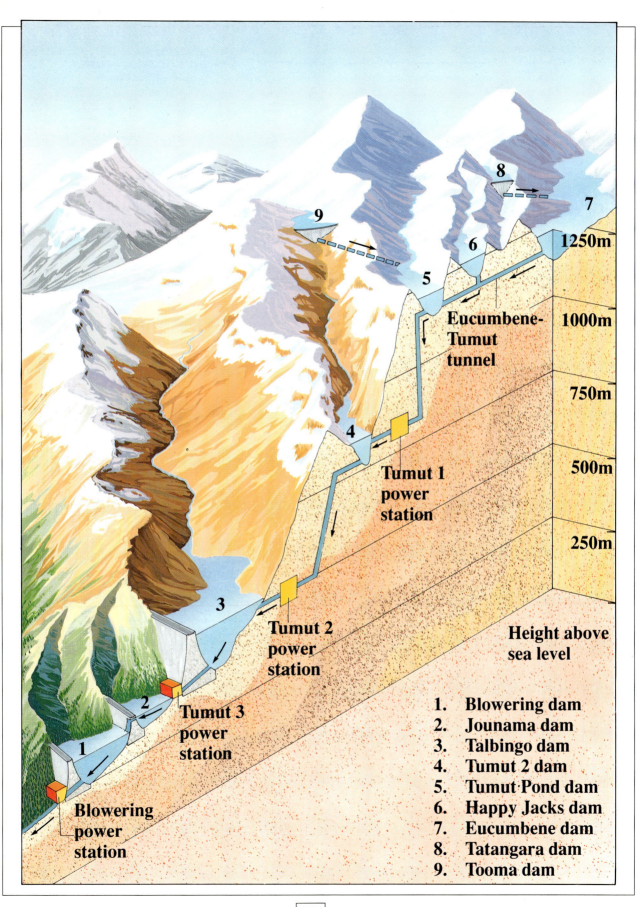

Making a water-wheel

Have fun making this water-wheel. You will need a grown-up to help you.

You need

4.5 volt electric motor or small dynamo, 1.5 volt light bulb, empty detergent bottle, 1 cork, 2 detergent bottle tops, electric wires, wire coat hanger, large gearwheel, small gearwheel, waterproof glue, 2 small blocks of wood, ball-point pen case, craft knife, sticky tape.

1. Cut off the bottom piece of the coat hanger. Push it through the cork until 1 cm is pushed right through.

2. Cut eight grooves lengthways in the cork. Glue in eight plastic strips cut from the detergent bottle.

3. Slide on the bottle tops and pen casing. Fix the large gearwheel on the end.

4. Tape the pen case to a block of wood. Place the block next to the sink so that the cork is under the tap (see main picture). Tape the block to the draining board.

5. Screw the motor to a block. Push the small gear on to the spindle. Connect up the motor and light bulb with the wires.

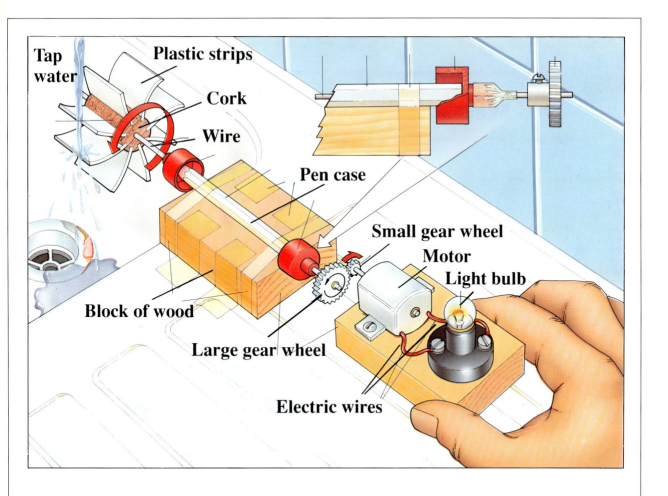

Turn on the tap so the water-wheel spins. Hold the block with the motor and press the small gear against the spinning large gear. The bulb should light up.

How it works

As the small gearwheel spins, the motor acts like a generator and sends a current of electricity along the wires to light up the bulb.

The water-wheel may spray water everywhere! See if it works in the bath. If not, use the sink and move or cover up anything near that could get wet.

Glossary

Acid rain A kind of pollution that falls in rain.

Barrage A long wall built across an estuary to hold back water.

Dam A wall built across a river to hold back water.

Developed countries Rich countries.

Developing countries Poor countries.

Environment The world around us. For example, animals, plants, mountains and rivers.

Estuary The widest part of a river, where it meets the sea.

Fossil fuels Gas, coal and oil that have formed from the remains of plants and animals that lived millions of year ago.

Generator A machine that makes electricity.

Gravity The pulling force of the Earth, Moon and Sun.

Hydroelectric power station A power station where electricity is made from falling water. It includes a dam, tunnels, turbines and generators.

Kilowatt One thousand watts, or units of electricity. One kilowatt has enough power for a one-bar electric heater.

Kinetic energy The energy in moving water.

Megawatt One million watts, or units of electricity.

Reservoir A lake made by people.

Sluice gates Gates in a barrage or dam that can be raised or lowered.

Turbines Machines that turn to drive generators.

Further Reading

Energy by Deborah Elliott (Wayland, 1993)

Power by Julie Brown and Robert Brown (Belitha Press, 1991)

My Science Book of Electricity by Neil Ardley (Dorling Kindersley, 1991)

My Science Book of Energy by Neil Ardley (Dorling Kindersley, 1992)

My Science Book of Water by Neil Ardley (Dorling Kindersley, 1991)

Science with Water (Usborne, 1992)

Where does Electricity Come From? by Susan Mayes (Usborne, 1989)

Index

Acid rain 4
Australia 25

Barrage 11

Coal 4, 5

Dam 8, 21, 26

Electricity 5, 6, 8, 24, 26
Environment 5
Estuary 11, 12

Fossil fuels 5

Gas 4, 5, 19
Generator 21
Gravity 10

Hydroelectric power 8, 21, 22, 23

Kinetic energy 6, 7, 14

Oceans 6, 10, 14, 18, 19
Oil 4, 5

Power stations 5, 12, 16, 22, 23, 26

Reservoirs 8, 9, 21
Rivers 6, 8, 11, 12, 25, 26

Seas 11, 17
  heat from 18-19
Snowy Mountains scheme 25-6
Streams 6, 25

Tides 10
  power from 11-12
Turbines 11, 14, 19, 21, 24

Waterfalls 6
Water-wheel 7, 8,
  making a 28-9
Waves 14-17